WITHDRAWN

Pebble™ Plus

Healthy Eating with MyPyramid

The Meat and Beans Group

by Mari C. Schuh

Consulting Editor: Gail Saunders-Smith, PhD

Consultant: Barbara J. Rolls, PhD
Guthrie Chair in Nutrition
The Pennsylvania State University
University Park, Pennsylvania

Capstone press
Mankato, Minnesota

Pebble Plus is published by Capstone Press,
151 Good Counsel Drive, P.O. Box 669, Mankato, Minnesota 56002.
www.capstonepress.com

1 2 3 4 5 6 11 10 09 08 07 06

Library of Congress Cataloging-in-Publication Data
Schuh, Mari C., 1975–
    The meat and beans group / by Mari C. Schuh.
    p. cm.—(Pebble Plus. Healthy eating with MyPyramid)
    Includes bibliographical references and index.
    Summary: "Simple text and photographs present the meat and beans group, the foods in this group, and
examples of healthy eating choices"—Provided by publisher.
    ISBN-13: 978-0-7368-5372-9 (hardcover)
    ISBN-10: 0-7368-5372-3 (hardcover)
    1. Meat—Juvenile literature. 2. Beans—Juvenile literature. 3. Nutrition—Juvenile literature. I. Title.
II. Series.
TX373.S38 2006
641.2'82—dc22   2005023704

Credits
Jennifer Bergstrom, designer; Kelly Garvin, photo researcher; Stacy Foster and Michelle Biedscheid,
    photo shoot coordinators

Photo Credits
Capstone Press/Karon Dubke, all except U.S. Department of Agriculture, 8 (inset), 9 (computer screen)

The author dedicates this book to meat lovers Chantill and Tom Kahler-Royer of North Mankato, Minnesota.

Capstone Press thanks Hilltop Hy-Vee employees in Mankato, Minnesota, for their helpful assistance with
photo shoots.

**Information in this book supports the U.S. Department of Agriculture's MyPyramid for Kids
food guidance system found at http://www.MyPyramid.gov/kids. Food amounts listed in this
book are based on an 1,800-calorie food plan.**

**The U.S. Department of Agriculture (USDA) does not endorse any products, services,
or organizations.**

Note to Parents and Teachers

The Healthy Eating with MyPyramid set supports national science standards related to
nutrition and physical health. This book describes and illustrates the meat and beans
group. The images support early readers in understanding the text. The repetition of
words and phrases helps early readers learn new words. This book also introduces early
readers to subject-specific vocabulary words, which are defined in the Glossary section.
Early readers may need assistance to read some words and to use the Table of Contents,
Glossary, Read More, Internet Sites, and Index sections of the book.

Table of Contents

The Meat and Beans Group

Have you eaten

any foods from the

meat and beans group today?

Meat, chicken, fish.

Beans, eggs, nuts, and seeds.

These foods give you protein.

MyPyramid for Kids

MyPyramid is a tool
to help you eat healthy food.
The meat and beans group
is part of MyPyramid.

To learn more about
healthy eating,
go to this web site:
www.MyPyramid.gov/kids
Ask an adult for help.

9

Eat 5 ounces from
the meat and beans group
every day.

Enjoying Meat and Beans

Some meats have lots of fat.

Low-fat meats are

better for you.

Choose low-fat beef, chicken,

pork, turkey, and fish.

Meats! Mankato's Finest Quality Meats! Manka
LEAN GROUND BEEF
93/7
FRESHNESS GUARANTEED
HONEYSUCKLE WHITE
DINNER'S ALMOST READY
Breast

Yum! Enjoy a sandwich
at lunch. If you want
to try a new food,
have a veggie burger.

Brrrrr! Warm up
with a bowl of chili
on a cold night.
Dig into the spicy meat
and beans.

Mixed nuts

make a crunchy snack.

Nuts have protein

and give you energy.

Foods from the

meat and beans group

are part of a healthy meal.

What are your favorites?

How Much to Eat

Many kids need to eat 5 ounces from the meat and beans group every day. To get 5 ounces, pick five of your favorite foods below.

Pick five foods below to eat today!

1 ounce of baked beans

½ ounce of sunflower seeds

1 ounce of shrimp

½ veggie burger

1 tablespoon of peanut butter

1 egg

1 ounce of tuna

1 slice of lean turkey

Glossary

energy—the strength to do active things without getting tired

MyPyramid—a food plan that helps kids make healthy food choices and reminds kids to be active; MyPyramid was created by the U.S. Department of Agriculture.

protein—a substance found in plant and animal cells; your body needs protein to work right.

Read More

Klingel, Cynthia Fitterer, and Robert B. Noyed. *Meat.* Let's Read About Food. Milwaukee: Weekly Reader Early Learning Library, 2002.

Rondeau, Amanda. *Proteins Are Powerful.* What Should I Eat? Edina, Minn.: Abdo, 2003.

Thomas, Ann. *Meat and Protein.* Food. Philadelphia: Chelsea Clubhouse, 2003.

Index

Word Count: 142
Grade: 1
Early-Intervention Level: 15

Internet Sites

FactHound offers a safe, fun way to find Internet sites related to this book. All of the sites on FactHound have been researched by our staff.

Here's how:

1. Visit *www.facthound.com*

2. Type in this special code **0736853723** for age-appropriate sites. Or enter a search word related to this book for a more general search.

3. Click on the **Fetch It** button.

FactHound will fetch the best sites for you!